Fig.1.

W9-BLJ-466

Good Question!

What Sank the World's Biggest Ship?

AND OTHER QUESTIONS ABOUT . . .

The Titanic

STERLING CHILDREN'S BOOKS
New York

STERLING CHILDREN'S BOOKS
New York

An Imprint of Sterling Publishing
387 Park Avenue South
New York, NY 10016

STERLING CHILDREN'S BOOKS and the distinctive Sterling Children's Books logo are trademarks of Sterling Publishing Co., Inc.

Text © 2012 by Mary Kay Carson
Illustrations © 2012 Sterling Publishing Co., Inc.
Photo Credits: BNPS © bnps.co.uk, front endpaper right, 11; Corbis © The Mariners' Museum: title page, 5; © Ralph White: 13; © Bettmann: 27 top;
© Hulton-Deutsch Collection: front endpaper left top, 30 top; © Simon Kreitem/Reuters: 31 top; © Ralph White: bottom Getty Images © Hulton Archive/Getty Images: 19;
© Matt Campbell/AFP: 23 left; © Universal Images Group: front endpaper left bottom, 23 right, 27 bottom; © Topical Press Agency: 27 middle; Bob Thomas/Popperfoto: 30 bottom

All rights reserved. No part of this publication may be reproduced, stored in a retrieval system, or transmitted, in any form or by any means,
electronic, mechanical, photocopying, recording, or otherwise, without prior written permission from the publisher.

ISBN 978-1-4027-8733-1 (PB)
ISBN 978-1-4027-9627-2 (HC)

Library of Congress Cataloging-in-Publication Data
Carson, Mary Kay.
 What sank the world's biggest ship? : and other questions about the
Titanic / by Mary Kay Carson.
 p. cm. -- (Who knew?)
 ISBN 978-1-4027-8733-1
 1. Titanic (Steamship)--Juvenile literature. 2. Shipwrecks--North Atantic
Ocean--Juvenile literature. I. Title.
 G530.T6.C365 2012
 910.9163'4--dc22

2011019964

Distributed in Canada by Sterling Publishing
^C/o Canadian Manda Group, 165 Dufferin Street
Toronto, Ontario, Canada M6K 3H6
Distributed in the United Kingdom by GMC Distribution Services
Castle Place, 166 High Street, Lewes, East Sussex, England BN7 1XU
Distributed in Australia by Capricorn Link (Australia) Pty. Ltd.
P.O. Box 704, Windsor, NSW 2756, Australia

Design by Merideth Harte
Paintings by Mark Elliot

For information about custom editions, special sales, and premium and corporate purchases, please contact
Sterling Special Sales at 800-805-5489 or specialsales@sterlingpublishing.com.

Manufactured in China
Lot #:
2 4 6 8 10 9 7 5 3 1
01/12

www.sterlingpublishing.com/kids

CONTENTS

What sank the world's biggest ship?

The *Titanic* is a legendary steamship. It's been famous for more than a century. On April 10, 1912, the giant ship left on her first voyage. It was also her last voyage. For its time, the *Titanic* was the largest passenger ship in the world. Some 2,200 people were onboard—among them were celebrities, millionaires, and royalty. If you wanted to travel in luxury, the *Titanic* was the way to go. No other ocean liner had such elegant rooms and fancy food. The *Titanic* was also the safest ship around. Its high-tech design was called unsinkable, but the *Titanic* did sink. It hit an iceberg and dropped to the bottom of the sea. More than 1,500 people died.

Mysteries and myths soon sprang up around the ship's sinking. Tales of rescue and tragedy on the *Titanic* filled newspapers and magazines. Survivors described how the ship sank. But eyewitnesses did not agree. Some said the iceberg punched a hole in the *Titanic*. Others said that the ship broke in two. Rumors spread that the lookout crew didn't have binoculars. Was the *Titanic* going too fast? Did an iceberg sink the *Titanic*? Or did a chain of mistakes doom the ship? And what was it like to be there?

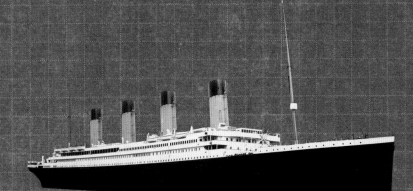

Why was the *Titanic* so big?

You could easily get lost on the *Titanic*. It was *that* big. The 882-foot (269 m) ship was as long as four city blocks, and as wide as eight highway lanes. There were nine decks, or levels, from top to bottom. In 1912, an ocean liner was the only way to get from Europe to America. Airplane travel would not become popular for several decades. The North Atlantic Ocean was a watery highway between continents. Companies in England were making bigger and faster ships to carry people and goods back and forth. Many Europeans were moving to America—they were called immigrants.

Moving so many people and so much stuff across an ocean takes a powerful motor. Huge furnaces and coal filled the *Titanic's* lowest deck. The ship's engines burned 650 tons of coal each day, and the smoke rose through its four six-story high smoke stacks. The *Titanic* plowed ahead at up to 24 miles (39 km) per hour. That was pretty fast, considering that it weighed 46,000 tons—more than 200 train engines. The *Titanic* was named after giant Greek gods called titans. The ship certainly earned her name. At the time, it was the largest human-made moving object in the world.

Why did everyone think the *Titanic* was unsinkable?

The *Titanic* was high-tech for its time. It had a double-layered bottom. Steel walls divided the below-water part of the ship into sixteen separate compartments. If the outside, or hull, of the ship sprang a leak, watertight doors closed off that compartment so the entire ship wouldn't flood. The *Titanic* was designed to be unsinkable. It would stay afloat even if water filled four of the sixteen compartments. Travelers wanted to cross the Atlantic Ocean in the safe, new, unsinkable ship. Who wouldn't?

The *Titanic* was not as safe as it could have been, though. Unsinkable or not, ocean liners had to have lifeboats. Emergencies happen. The rule was at least sixteen lifeboats per ship. The ship designer wanted forty-eight lifeboats, but that many lifeboats took up a lot of space. The ship company did not want all those boats on the deck. Besides, the ocean liner was designed to be safe. So many lifeboats weren't necessary. Builders put in only twenty lifeboats.

Did cheap parts help sink the *Titanic*?

Three thousand workers spent nearly three years building the gigantic ocean liner. The propellers were as wide as houses. The smokestacks were like farm silos. Overlapping steel plates formed the ship's outer hull. Big metal bolts, called rivets, fastened the inch-thick plates together. Workers hammered millions of sausage-sized rivets into the hull. The tops, or heads, of the rivets are round like mushroom caps. The round bumps on the hull are the heads of rivets.

The strongest rivets are steel. But iron rivets were easier to hammer into place. The ship company did not buy the strongest iron rivets available, however. In 1998, undersea explorers collected iron rivets from the sunken *Titanic*. When metal experts studied them, they found a problem. The rivets were made of cheap, weak iron. The iceberg scraped the rivet heads right off the hull. With the rivets broken, the hull plates came apart. And seawater flooded in. Using cheap rivets likely cost 1,500 lives.

Where were the ship's binoculars?

Last minute changes can create problems.

The captain chosen for the *Titanic*'s first, or maiden, voyage was Edward John Smith. He was called the Millionaire's Captain. Why? Because rich passengers liked him. Some even requested Smith's ships when traveling. Smith captained ships for twenty-five years. He planned to retire after the *Titanic*'s maiden voyage. He didn't get the chance.

Before the *Titanic* started its trip, Captain Smith made a last minute change to the crew. Officer David Blair was replaced. In a rush to leave the ship, Blair forgot to turn in a key to a locker. The locker stored binoculars for the lookout crew. As Blair got off the *Titanic*, hundreds of other workers got on. More than six hundred men and women worked on the ship. There were bellboys, cooks, sailors, engineers, coal stokers, and stewards. But no one missed the locker key until the ship was at sea.

Which month has the most icebergs?

Around the time the *Titanic*'s designer was rethinking lifeboats, a two-million-ton piece of a Greenland glacier broke off. The 10,000-year-old hunk of snow and ice fell into the ocean. An iceberg was born. By 1912, it was moving in an ice field with other icebergs and floating ice. Spring is when the ice fields float south and get in the way of ships. Ocean liners crossing the North Atlantic have to watch out for icebergs, especially in April. That's the month with the most icebergs about.

On April 10, 1912, the *Titanic* launched from England. It was a Wednesday. The ship stopped in France and Ireland before heading to the open Atlantic on Thursday. The passengers settled in, finding ways to pass the time. The ship was expected to arrive in New York on Monday, April 15. By the *Titanic*'s first day in the open sea, warnings were coming in. Nearby ships were seeing icebergs.

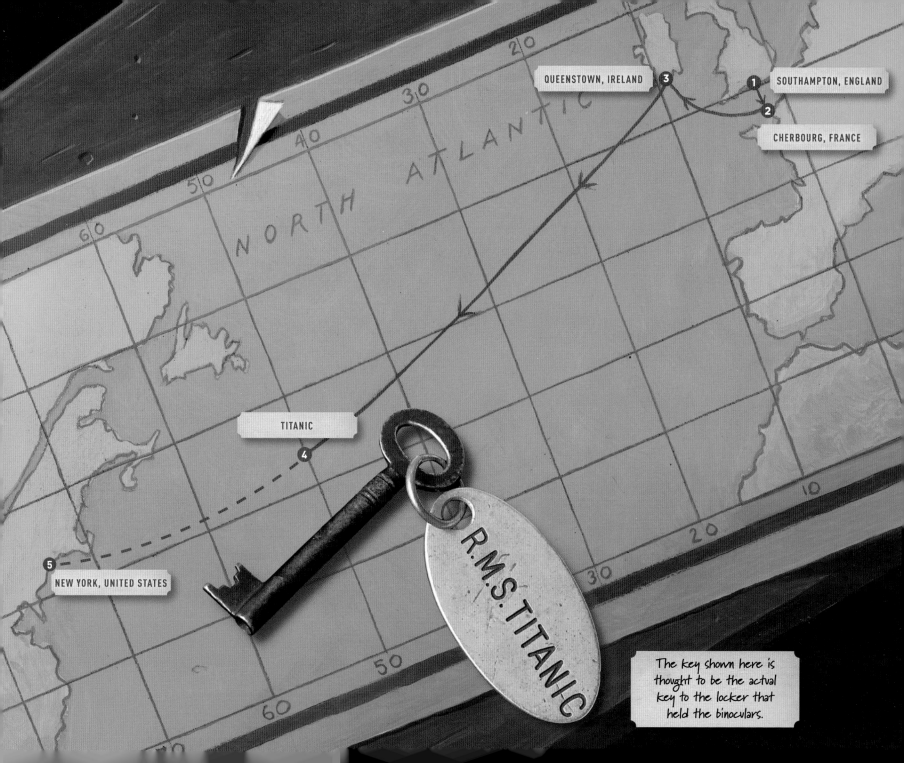

QUEENSTOWN, IRELAND **3**

1 SOUTHAMPTON, ENGLAND

2 CHERBOURG, FRANCE

NORTH ATLANTIC

TITANIC **4**

5 NEW YORK, UNITED STATES

R.M.S. TITANIC

The key shown here is thought to be the actual key to the locker that held the binoculars.

What was it like to travel first class aboard the *Titanic*?

Three classes of passengers sailed on the *Titanic*. Each had a very different trip on the ship. The classes did not mix. Dining, lounge, and deck areas were separated by class.

How passengers boarded the *Titanic* was separated by class, too. A wealthy businessman traveling first class entered the *Titanic* on an upper deck. Ship staff greeted him and guided him to his room. His $430 ticket got him a big private room. He wore formal clothes while eating lobster, steak, and fancy desserts. Musicians played outside the elegant dining room during the seven-course meal. What else could he do onboard? He might swim in the pool, exercise in the gym, send telegraph messages to friends, or develop photographs in the darkroom.

Second-class travelers got less luxury. A $65 ticket bought a comfortable hotel-like room. Two to four passengers slept in each. Waiters served four-course dinners in the second-class dining room. Passengers read in the library. They played games like chess and dominoes in the second-class lounges. Men could visit the barbershop.

A family traveling third class entered the ship on a lower deck. A medical officer met them. Only healthy immigrants could enter the United States. What did a $35 ticket buy? A bunk bed in a room shared with many people and three meals each day. Third-class passengers mostly made their own fun. They brought out their own instruments and sang and danced. The top deck at the back of the ship, called the poop deck, was open to third-class passengers. Kids played games outside and swung on ropes. Others walked in the chilly sea air.

Second-class boat deck aboard the *Titanic*.

Did the telegraph operator ignore an important message?

Titanic's telephones couldn't call off the ship. Any messages between ships and to land were sent with telegraph signals. Telegraph operators tapped out words and sentences in a code of dots and dashes. By noon on Sunday, April 14, nearby ships had sent warnings. Icebergs were around. Later that day, other ships sent more messages. Icebergs had been spotted in the Titanic's path.

The closest ship sent an emergency ice warning just before 11:00 p.m. The Californian said it was stopping for the night. Crossing the ice field was too dangerous in the dark. Jack Phillips, Titanic's telegraph operator, got the message. It came while he was very busy. He had so many passenger messages to tap out. And the ship would be out of radio range soon. Being interrupted by the Californian's warning made him angry. Frustrated, he told the Californian to stop sending messages. The Titanic's nearest neighbor turned off its radio for the night.

How could an iceberg appear out of nowhere?

Two lookout crewmen watched for ice all night. The night of April 14th was cold, clear, calm and without moonlight. The crewmen peered hard out at the dark sea, looking for ice. The water was flat and smooth, like glass. If there had been waves, they might have splashed against an iceberg and alerted the crewmen. But the calm water slipped unseen around everything in the ocean that night.

Binoculars would have helped the lookouts see farther. But the crewmen couldn't open the locker where they were kept. The key was hundreds of miles away. Captain Smith knew icebergs were around, but he didn't want to arrive late in New York. The Titanic raced through the night at full speed.

The iceberg came into view all of a sudden. It was only a football field away. Right away, the lookouts rang the emergency bell three times. The signal meant danger. At 11:40 p.m., lookout Fred Fleet told the crew that there was an iceberg right ahead. The icy monster was huge—most of it was hidden underwater.

Did the *Titanic* crash into the iceberg?

The sound of serious orders filled the dark, chilly *Titanic* bridge. *Hard-a-starboard! Reverse engines! Seal off the compartments!* Crewmen steered the ship away from the iceberg. The ocean liner turned slowly, like a sleepy giant. A long thirty-seven seconds ticked by. The *Titanic* was swerving away. Might the ship slip past the iceberg? Then the *Titanic* shuddered. An underwater wedge of ice was scraping the front hull. This was one of the curved parts held together with weak iron rivets. The iceberg shaved the rivet heads off the hull one after another as the *Titanic* slid by. Free of rivets, the steel plates pulled apart. The hull opened like a zipper as long as a football field.

The first six watertight compartments gulped in the Atlantic Ocean. Icy water drenched men shoveling coal into fiery furnaces. Seven tons of seawater flooded in with every passing second. The water filled the sealed compartments, where hundreds of men were trapped. And they weren't the only ones doomed. Six flooded compartments were two too many. The *Titanic* could not stay afloat with more than four flooded compartments. The ship's pumps sucked out seawater. But the water overpowered the pumps. They couldn't keep up. Too much water was coming in.

Did the passengers panic?

Not right away. Passengers only felt the ship shake a bit. There was no big crash. Many slept through it. Most of those who were awake when it happened were not worried—at first. The *Titanic* was unsinkable, after all! The band kept playing.

Captain Smith was worried. He instantly left his room and rushed onto the bridge, asking what they had struck. An iceberg. The captain went below to check for damage. The mailroom was flooded. Papers and envelopes floated out of sorting slots. Seawater was filling the hull compartments opened up by the iceberg. The pumps were not keeping up. Captain Smith could already feel the front of the ship, the bow, pulling down. The *Titanic* was going to sink—soon. They'd stay afloat maybe a couple of hours. Calling for help was all they could do.

The *Californian* was only two hours away. But it was not answering any calls. Its radio was silent. What ship was the next closest? The *Carpathia* answered. It instantly turned toward the *Titanic* at full speed. Captain Smith knew, though, that the rescue ship wouldn't make it. Not in time, anyway— the *Carpathia* was four hours away. That meant 2,200 people were going to have to abandon ship.

Why didn't everyone just get in the lifeboats?

Stewards woke up passengers. Sleepy families in pajamas and coats gathered on deck. Some wore life jackets. Crewmen began loading lifeboats with mostly women and children. A lifeboat didn't seem like a safe idea to some. Many still believed the *Titanic* wouldn't sink. Better to wait on the ship for rescue.

Around 12:45 a.m. movie star Dorothy Gibson got into the first lifeboat with only eighteen others. Each lifeboat could carry sixty-five people. Soon the *Titanic*'s deck grew more slanted from the sinking bow. Panic set in. Lifeboats filled up quickly and fully. Terrified passengers realized what the crew already knew. There were not enough lifeboats. People were going to be left behind. And the *Titanic* was not unsinkable.

People tried jumping into full boats. Gunshots sounded. An officer fired in the air to try to keep order. By 2:00 a.m., the last lifeboat was gone. More than 1,500 people were still onboard. The *Titanic* sent out frantic final messages: *We are sinking fast. Women and children in boats. Cannot last much longer.*

This drawing from 1912 shows lifeboats from the *Titanic* being lowered into the water.

What did the people left behind do?

Captain Smith knew there was nothing more he or his crew could do. The *Titanic*'s captain walked away and was never seen again. Seawater soon swamped the bridge. A priest tried to comfort those gathered on deck. The ship's band played. Some passengers returned to their rooms. Others tied deck chairs together to make rafts. Waves rolled over the sinking bow, sweeping people into the sea. The thick wires holding the first smokestack snapped. The giant tube of metal broke off and slammed into the sea. The *Titanic*'s water-filled bow dove down. The ship's back, or stern, rose up out of the sea. Those huddled in lifeboats watched the propellers turning in the air.

Why did the *Titanic* crack in two?

A roar came from the ship. The horrible sound of sliding furniture, breaking plates, tumbling cargo, and falling people. Everything and everyone went crashing forward. The sea swallowed the bow, and the stern lifted farther up out of the water. All the heavy engines were in the back of the ship. Their tremendous weight pulled the stern back down toward the sea. This caused the hull to break in half, like a snapped pencil. The *Titanic* tore in two, right down the middle. The water-filled bow sank right away. The ripped-off stern settled back onto the water's surface. It bobbed for a few moments. Then water quickly rushed in, dragging it down to the bottom of the Atlantic Ocean. The *Titanic* was gone.

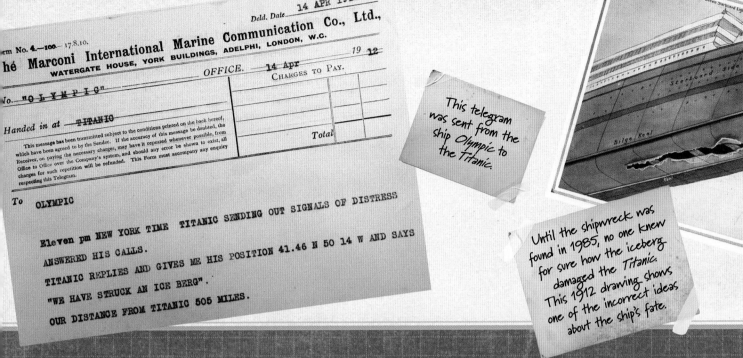

The Marconi International Marine Communication Co., Ltd.,
WATERGATE HOUSE, YORK BUILDINGS, ADELPHI, LONDON, W.C.

orm No. 4.—100—17.8.10.

Deld. Date. 14 APR 1912

No. "OLYMPIC"

OFFICE.   14 Apr   19 12

CHARGES TO PAY.

Handed in at   TITANIC

This message has been transmitted subject to the conditions printed on the back hereof, which have been agreed to by the Sender. If the accuracy of this message be doubted, the Receiver, on paying the necessary charges, may have it repeated whenever possible, from Office to Office over the Company's system, and should any error be shown to exist, all charges for such repetition will be refunded. This Form must accompany any enquiry respecting this Telegram.

Total

To   OLYMPIC

Eleven pm NEW YORK TIME TITANIC SENDING OUT SIGNALS OF DISTRESS
ANSWERED HIS CALLS.

TITANIC REPLIES AND GIVES ME HIS POSITION 41.46 N 50 14 W AND SAYS

"WE HAVE STRUCK AN ICE BERG".

OUR DISTANCE FROM TITANIC 505 MILES.

This telegram was sent from the ship *Olympic* to the *Titanic*.

Until the shipwreck was found in 1985, no one knew for sure how the iceberg damaged the *Titanic*. This 1912 drawing shows one of the incorrect ideas about the ship's fate.

What happened to the stranded passengers?

When the *Titanic* sank, 1,500 people went with it into the ocean. Some drowned trapped inside the ship. So did many people not wearing life jackets. But hundreds found themselves floating in an ocean of ice. They were not much better off. Air and water temperatures that April night were below freezing. Icy water can kill.

Freezing swimmers from the *Titanic* wailed and pleaded in the water. People in the lifeboats said the cries continued for up to an hour. Then the dark sea was quiet. Cold water caused the swimmers to lose consciousness. Why didn't those in the lifeboats help them? A few did. Survivors in a couple of lifeboats rowed back. They saved a half dozen or so swimmers. Most of the people in the lifeboats chose not to help. They feared that panicked swimmers might overturn the boats.

Did anyone survive?

Survivors huddled in lifeboats and waited for rescue. Some rowed their boats to warm themselves. A signal rocket streaked the sky around 3:30 a.m. The *Carpathia* was near. Rescue came too late for those in the water. Only baker Charles John Joughin survived being in the sea for hours. He claimed his belly full of whiskey saved him.

The rising sun turned the ice chunks pink and gold. The *Carpathia* hauled people out of lifeboats. Children were hoisted up in canvas bags. It was 8:30 a.m. before all were aboard. Shocked survivors lined the deck railing of the rescue ship. They watched each person come aboard from the final lifeboat. Hope left them. Whoever wasn't there now, was dead. Many burst into tears. They finally knew their husbands, sons, and friends hadn't made it. The *Carpathia* arrived in New York three days later. Thousands of people gathered to meet it. Were their loved ones among the 705 survivors?

Who lived and who died?

Chances of surviving the sinking *Titanic* were not equal. Women and children were loaded onto lifeboats first. Only one in five of the men on the *Titanic* survived. Nearly three-quarters of the women did. But only half of the children survived. Fifty-six kids died. They were not in lifeboats because they were down in third class. Only one in three kids in third class survived. All but one of the children traveling in first and second class lived. Third-class areas were deep in the ship. It was a long way up to the outside deck. The crew did not want panic, so some did not tell passengers the ship was sinking. Not everyone understood what was going on. Some immigrants did not speak English. Once people figured out what was happening, they headed for the deck. By then the lifeboats were full.

Lady Duff Gordon, *Titanic* passenger and survivor

Edward John Smith, Captain of the *Titanic*

This photograph shows *Titanic* survivors in lifeboats rowing to meet the *Carpathia*.

Did anybody get into trouble?

Whose fault was the *Titanic* tragedy? Who was to blame? Both Britain and the United States investigated. Questions were asked. Why was Captain Smith going so fast in an ice field? Why didn't the lookouts have binoculars? Why weren't there more lifeboats? Why didn't the *Californian* rescue them? Why was its radio turned off? Mistakes were surely made, but the crew hadn't broken laws. No one was arrested or sent to jail. But ships did change afterward. New designs had complete double hulls, not just double bottoms. The walls that separate the watertight compartments were made higher. They could be flooded longer without sinking. Ships carried enough lifeboats for everyone onboard. The International Ice Patrol was also created. To this day, it watches for icebergs in the North Atlantic.

Where is the *Titanic* now?

For more than seven decades, the *Titanic* was lost. Ships fighting in two world wars sailed above her. Jetliners began carrying passengers across the North Atlantic. Ocean liners mostly faded into history. But no one forgot about the *Titanic*. Many looked for the ship. Some wanted to raise the *Titanic* from the seafloor. In 1985, explorers found the *Titanic*. A small submarine videotaped the shipwreck site. It was 2.3 miles (3.8 km) underwater. The bow was 1,970 feet (600 m) from the stern. Finally, there was proof that the ship had broken in two. A year later, deep-water submarines with crews started visiting the wreck site. They found the stern smashed. But the bow was in one piece. Its railing dripped with rust. The *Titanic* had no hole or gash where the iceberg hit—just separated hull plates with missing rivets. Expeditions collected thousands of artifacts. Plates and cups, the crow's nest bell, luggage, shoes, and a piece of the hull, too.

SAVED FROM THE TITANIC

STARRING DOROTHY·GIBSON

ECLAIR FILM CO.

In this photograph from April 16, 1912, a boy in England sells newspapers about the *Titanic* tragedy.

TITANIC DISASTER GREAT LOSS OF LIFE
EVENING NEWS

WHITE STAR LINE

This postcard from 1911 shows an illustration of the *Titanic*.

After 100 years, why do people still care?

The *Titanic* was big news. The world's biggest ship had sunk—on its maiden voyage. An unsinkable ship went down after hitting an iceberg. Famous people and millionaires were lost at sea. Some 705 survivors lived to tell their tales. Survivor stories were everywhere. Newspapers and magazines printed their accounts. Movie star and *Titanic* survivor Dorothy Gibson made a silent film about it. She starred in *Saved from the Titanic* a month after the disaster! Movies, plays, songs, books, myths, mysteries, expeditions, and discoveries have kept *Titanic*'s story alive.

There are dozens of *Titanic* museums around the world. Historians keep studying the artifacts. Scientists test rivets and create computer images to understand how the ship sank. Scholars still argue about exactly what happened. There's no one left to ask. The last *Titanic* survivor passed away in 2009. Millvina Dean was a tiny baby on April 14, 1912. A crewman handed her in a sack to her mother as she got into a lifeboat. Dean and her family had left England to live in Missouri. They were traveling third class, deep in the ship. But as soon as they hit the iceberg, Dean's father got them up onto the deck. He never believed the great ship was unsinkable.

Millvina Dean was the last living survivor of the *Titanic*.

This underwater photograph shows the front of the *Titanic*.

TITANIC TIMELINE

1909 — THE *TITANIC* CONSTRUCTION BEGINS IN BELFAST, IRELAND. PARTS OF ITS HULL ARE FASTENED WITH CHEAP, WEAK IRON RIVETS.

1910 — A GIANT ICEBERG BREAKS FREE FROM A GREENLAND GLACIER. IT BEGINS MOVING SOUTH AND INTO THE *TITANIC*'S ROUTE. THE COMPANY BUILDING THE *TITANIC* DECIDES TO INSTALL ONLY 20 LIFEBOATS, INSTEAD OF 48.

1912

[APRIL 9] THE *TITANIC* OFFICER DAVID BLAIR IS REPLACED AT THE LAST MINUTE AND LEAVES THE SHIP. HE FORGETS TO TURN IN THE KEY TO THE LOOKOUT CREWS' LOCKER WHERE BINOCULARS ARE STORED.

[APRIL 11] THE *TITANIC* LEAVES ENGLAND FOR NEW YORK WITH 2,200 PEOPLE ONBOARD.

[APRIL 14] THE *TITANIC* RECEIVES ICEBERG WARNINGS THROUGHOUT THE DAY AND INTO THE EVENING, BUT CONTINUES ON COURSE AT FULL SPEED.

11:40 P.M. THE LOOKOUT CREW SPOTS A GIANT ICEBERG DEAD AHEAD. THE SHIP TRIES TO SWERVE AWAY. HOWEVER, LESS THAN A MINUTE LATER THE *TITANIC* SIDESWIPES THE ICEBERG, RIPPING OPEN PART OF ITS HULL. THE SHIP BEGINS TO SINK.

[APRIL 15]

12:00 A.M. CAPTAIN SMITH REALIZES THE *TITANIC* IS GOING TO SINK AND DISTRESS CALLS ARE SENT OUT. THE NEAREST SHIP TO ANSWER, THE *CARPATHIA*, IS FOUR HOURS AWAY.

12:25 A.M. CREW ORDERED TO BEGIN LOADING LIFEBOATS WITH WOMEN AND CHILDREN.

1:50 A.M. LAST LIFEBOAT LEAVES. 1,500 PEOPLE ARE STILL ONBOARD THE SINKING SHIP.

2:20 A.M. THE *TITANIC* BREAKS IN TWO AND SINKS TO THE BOTTOM OF THE OCEAN, SENDING HUNDREDS OF PEOPLE INTO THE ICY SEA.

4:00 A.M. THE *CARPATHIA* FINALLY ARRIVES AND RESCUES 705 SURVIVORS FROM THE LIFEBOATS.

[APRIL 18] THE *CARPATHIA* ARRIVES IN NEW YORK CITY WITH THE *TITANIC* SURVIVORS.

1985 — OCEAN EXPLORER ROBERT BALLARD DISCOVERS THE WRECK OF THE *TITANIC* ON THE OCEAN FLOOR.